Published in the UK by Scholastic Children's Books, 2020
Euston House, 24 Eversholt Street, London, NW1 1DB
A division of Scholastic Limited

London – New York – Toronto – Sydney – Auckland
Mexico City – New Delhi – Hong Kong

SCHOLASTIC and associated logos are trademarks and/or
registered trademarks of Scholastic Inc.

Written by Sara Conway © Scholastic Children's Books, 2020
Illustrations by Matthew Taylor Wilson © Scholastic Children's Books, 2020

ISBN 978 14071 9706 7

A CIP catalogue record for this book is available from the British Library.

All rights reserved.
This book is sold subject to the condition that it shall not, by way of trade or otherwise, be lent, hired out or otherwise circulated in any form of binding or cover other than that in which it is published. No part of this publication may be reproduced, stored in a retrieval system, or transmitted in any form or by any other means (electronic, mechanical, photocopying, recording or otherwise) without prior written permission of Scholastic Limited.

Any website addresses listed in the book are correct at the time of going to print. However, please be aware that online content is subject to change and websites can contain or offer content that is unsuitable for children. We advise all children be supervised when using the internet.

The publisher does not have any control over and does not assume any responsibility for the views, thoughts, and opinions of those individuals featured in this book.

Printed and bound in the UK by Bell and Bain Ltd, Glasgow
Papers used by Scholastic Children's Books are made
from wood grown in sustainable forests.

2 4 6 8 10 9 7 5 3 1

www.scholastic.co.uk

Sara Conway

Illustrated by
Matthew Taylor Wilson

■SCHOLASTIC

This book belongs to:

....

....

Contents

Welcome to YOUR book!   7
Every body is different   15
Keep calm and be kind   31
Yes, you can!   51
Take a bite out of life!   63
Squad goals   81
Keeping it real   97
Helping hand   109
Celebrate yourself   123
Being you begins with you   139
Glossary   154
Index   156
Where to find help   158

Welcome to YOUR book!

Meet the star of this book:

This book is like no other. Reading these pages could change your life. Do you know why? Because this book is all about

Usually, the star of the book is someone we get to know for a little while and then we say goodbye. Whether it's Harry Potter or Lyra Belacqua, when we close the last page, we wave them farewell. Not in this book. **YOU are the hero of this adventure**.

It doesn't matter whether you have straight hair or curly, brown eyes or blue. Whether you're into sport, movies or reading. This book doesn't care what trainers you're wearing, if you scored a goal or if you passed a test. **YOU** have the power to be anything you want to be. This book is about finding out what makes YOU amazing.

'ME?' You might ask. **'What's so special about me?'** The answer to that is everything! Look in the mirror. Tilt your head this way and that way. Cross your eyes, stick out your tongue and give a big cheesy grin. That person smiling back at you is unique from head to toe. There's no one exactly like you on this earth. *No one*. Not a single person. Isn't that crazy?

Let's prove it

Fill in these facts about you...

My name is:

....

This is who is in my family:

....
....

My shoe size is:

....

I like watching:

....

My favourite book is:

....

The funniest thing I can do is:

....

I am awesome because:

....
....

What's inside?

Books take you on exciting journeys. They make you care about the hero and want them to succeed. Sometimes, they can even help you see things from another point of view. This book is no different. And remember – the **hero** of this story is **YOU**!

Of course, every good adventure would be ruined if you found out the ending on page one. So, we won't tell you exactly what you'll be doing on your journey. But we will give you a hint of what you'll learn along the way…

You and your body will become best friends.

You'll thank your body for helping you do amazing things.

You'll discover your secret superpower and use it to make you – and others – feel awesome.

You'll meet some superfoods and learn some super moves!

You'll learn how to be web wise and social media smart.

You'll find out how to keep it real.

You'll feel confident to deal with whatever life throws your way.

There's no time like now!

These chapters are created to help you feel happier and more confident in your own body. The topics they cover will be useful today, tomorrow and the next day, in fact, for the rest of your life!

Body confidence isn't something we are born with. It doesn't matter who we are or what we look like – the truth is we *all* need a little help to feel comfortable in our own skin. It's easy to tell someone else that they did a good job, or they look nice, or they deserve a rest. But, for some reason, we struggle to say these things to ourselves. Even grown-ups find it hard to be kind to themselves every day. **But it IS possible to learn** – and, just like riding a bike, with a little practice it becomes easy and you never forget how.

Learning these skills now is so important. Feeling confident from head to toe will make you braver, smarter and stronger. It will help you to be true to yourself and to achieve your dreams.

It's okay to ask for help

This book introduces topics that you might not have thought about before and it touches on big themes, like bullying and growing up. Some of these issues might make you feel confused or even a little worried. If reading this book is making you feel wobbly then it's a good idea to talk to someone about how you're feeling. You know who you feel most comfortable with – it might be your mum or dad, but it's okay if it's someone else like a teacher, a mentor at school, a family member or even your friend's mum or dad. Remember, every adventure has its ups and downs. Just setting off on this journey proves how brave you are.

Get ready!

There's one easy thing you can do now to prepare for what lies ahead. Look in the mirror again and, this time, say something nice to yourself. It might help to pretend you're talking to a friend. You might say, **'I like your hair,' 'You're clever'** or **'I really like that thing you did today!'** Now say another kind thing, and another, until the compliments are rolling off your tongue. See? **You're amazing**!

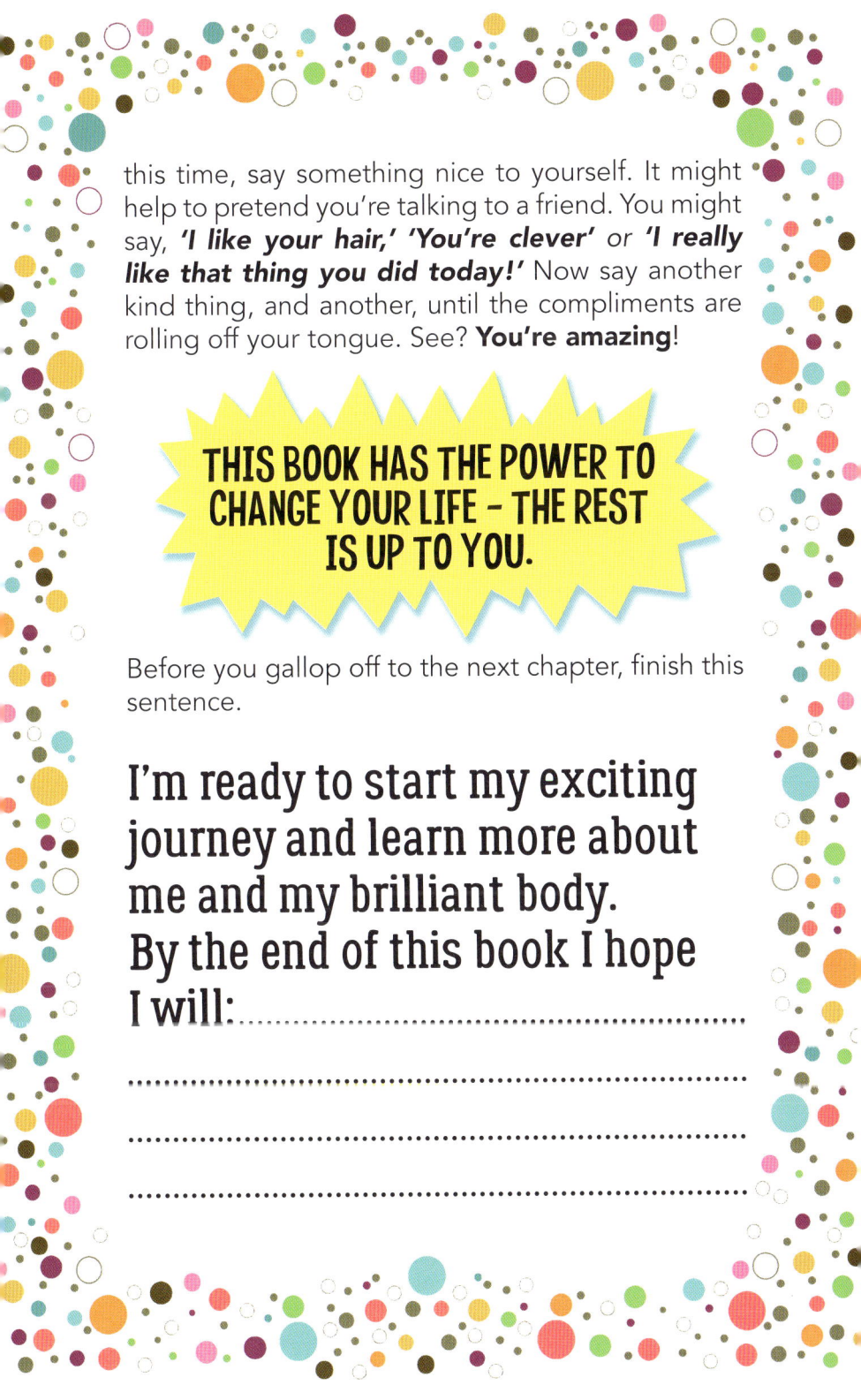

THIS BOOK HAS THE POWER TO CHANGE YOUR LIFE – THE REST IS UP TO YOU.

Before you gallop off to the next chapter, finish this sentence.

I'm ready to start my exciting journey and learn more about me and my brilliant body. By the end of this book I hope I will:..

....

....

....

LOVE YOURSELF FROM HEAD TO TOE

Every body is DIFFERENT

Welcome to chapter two! When did you last say thank you to your amazing body? What's that? You never have? Well, maybe it's time you stopped to consider all of the incredible things your body does for you. Like, helping you to read this book right now. Over the next few pages, you'll discover what makes YOUR body special, plus, you'll visit a desert island and learn a special mind trick. Let's go!

Your body is brilliant

Whether you're running, dancing, eating, chatting, hugging or lying down doing nothing at all, your body is constantly working to help you be YOU. Think about your favourite hobby. Maybe you love playing football. To line up the perfect goal, you need to use your brain, your eyes, your mean kick – and every muscle in between – to keep you moving, balancing and aiming right at the back of the net. And what part of your body gets to nap while you're busy being brilliant? Er, none of it, that's what!

Even when you're asleep, your body is downloading everything you learned that day and resetting itself ready for tomorrow. Every hour of every day, your body does something amazing for you. So, give yourself a big pat on the back and say thank you to your body for doing its amazing job.

Your body is unique

Some of us are better at singing than doing the long jump, or prefer studying the stars to playing the drums – and that's okay, because every body is different. Let's imagine a world where everyone looks the same and has the same talents. We'll call these people the Bobs.

Meet the BoBs

The Bobs are an average height and an average build. They have average colour hair and average colour eyes. Oh, and they all love fishing.

The Bobs would get boring, very quickly*.

Now, we're going to imagine this bunch of Bobs are stranded on a desert island. **'I'll catch some fish!'** say all of the Bobs. And the Bobs catch hundreds of fish. But no one knows how to cook the fish, how to find drinking water or how to build a shelter. And they certainly don't know how to deal with spiders or sunburn or killer sharks. The Bobs are stranded

* We've got nothing against Bobs. Or fishing for that matter.

with nothing to eat or drink, nowhere to sleep, a big pile of smelly fish and **KILLER SHARKS**?

The Bobs wouldn't be great for the survival of the human race, either. It's the things we all do differently and our unique skills that make the world so much more **amazing**.

I bet your friendship group is filled with people who are tall, short or somewhere in between. You have different coloured hair and eyes. Maybe you have things in common, like knowing all the words to your favourite songs. But some of you will love maths, others will love art or music or languages. Some of you are good at talking, others at listening and others at making everyone else laugh. If your crew got stranded on a desert island, you'd survive because you'd each bring your own special skills. Think again about those hobbies you love. They're a big part of what makes you YOU. And your own unique body makes them possible. Time for another big pat on the back.

On the next page, stick in a photo or drawing of yourself.

Now, label the different parts of your body and write down the brilliant things they do for you.

Not sure what to write? Here's some helpful hints! You might label your goal-scoring legs and feet, your clever fingers that help you to draw or write, or your amazing mouth that helps you to speak, laugh and taste birthday cakes. It's your body, so write whatever makes you feel happy!

Every body is normal

Now we know why it is important for everyone to be different, it's easy to see that every type of body is normal. But what's weird is that when you look at famous people on television or in magazines, you don't often see different body shapes. In fact, you don't see faces from many different cultures or people with disabilities either. And the celebrities look a little bit too perfect. Their skin seems to glow, their clothes always look amazing and they never have a hair out of place.

The problem is, when we see these images over and over again, we start to think what we're seeing IS normal. And we might worry there's something wrong with us if we don't look like celebrities. We'll be chatting about this some more in chapter six, but the important thing to know now is that you, your classmates and everyone on the street – you're REAL. And, just like when you watch cartoons, most of what you see on TV isn't real at all. Your favourite stars can still inspire you – you can sing along with their songs and watch their movies. But it's good to remember that no one is perfect. Sometimes, celebrities get bogies hanging out of their noses or their hair sticks out of place. We just don't see that very often.

Every body changes

So, you've got to know your body. You're a team. You love hanging out together and doing the stuff

you love to do. And then, overnight, your body gets a little bit different. Now feels like a good time to talk about puberty. You may have heard of it and be wondering what's going to happen. Or you might be thinking, **'My BBF (best body forever) is about to do what?'** Just to make sure we're all on the same page, here's a quick lowdown on what to expect.

The most important things you need to know are:

Puberty is normal.
Everyone goes through it.
You will be fine. Phew!

What is puberty?

Puberty is an important part of growing up, that will transform you into an adult. It affects everyone differently – boys and girls go through different changes, but no two girls or two boys develop at the same rate. Remember what we agreed about every body being different and every body being normal? The same goes for the way we experience puberty.

What will happen to me?

The first changes are hidden inside your body when new hormones start whizzing around. Their job is to send messages to different parts of your body telling them to grow or behave in a slightly different way. You'll have no idea that this is happening at first. Then, one day, you might start to notice changes.

You might find you grow a lot taller all at once. You might need new jeans – result!

You'll start to notice hair growing in different places and your body shape will start to change.

You might also find you feel tired and grumpy or a little sad, and that's normal, too.

The good thing is many of these changes are hidden from the outside world, so only you will know they're happening. That means you can get used to them at your own pace. That said, you might find you grow before – or after – your friends, which might make you feel a little self-conscious. But, everyone is different and we all get there. Be kind to yourself as your body is working hard to help you grow up to be an adult.

If you find yourself feeling worried or just want some more information about what's going on, talk to a trusted adult. And remember everyone is bound to be feeling a little weird about the changes they're going through – even if they don't show it. Talk to your friends and be kind to other people around you. And, remember, no matter how much you tell your friends, your body is private. You don't have to show or share anything with anyone if you don't want to.

How can I help my body?

We've talked about the ways your body grows all by itself, but your body also changes when you treat it differently. You can make yourself faster, stronger and more skilful if you practise moving in new ways.

Imagine you're learning a new dance routine. At first, it seems impossible that you'll be able to do the whole dance to music without bumping into someone or tripping over your feet. But, when you break the dance down into manageable chunks and you practise those sections over and over again, something amazing happens. Your body remembers how to move without you having to think about it at all. And, as well as picking up the steps, your muscles grow stronger and more flexible to allow you to move to the rhythm without breaking a sweat.

The same goes for horse riding and hockey, drawing and drama, even knitting and beekeeping. The more you do something, the better you become. And your body changes to help you be the best you can be.

Train your brain

Your brain is a muscle and you can train it, too. Try this fun challenge to improve your memory.

First of all, read this list of objects, and then hide the page and see how many you can remember – without peeking. Try to say them in order if you can.

teddy	kite
apple	ham sandwich
key	torch
bouncy ball	

Tricky, isn't it? But not if you try this amazing method.

Close your eyes and imagine that you are walking around your home. As you go, leave the objects in different places. Hug your teddy and leave it on your bed. Walk into the kitchen and take a bite out of the apple. Insert the key in the back door. You get the idea. The important thing is to really visualize each object before you leave it.

Now, retrace your steps and see how many objects you can remember. Was it a lot easier than the first time? The great thing is, you'll be able to return to your home in your mind and recall the list tomorrow and in a few days time. Use this new skill to impress a friend (don't tell them your trick at first!) It could also help you to revise for tests! Change the location for each new list – your school, your friend's house or a grandparent's – anywhere you know really well.

Every body is surprising

Your body doesn't make a big song and dance about the things it can do (unless your talent is singing and dancing, of course). You can appear athletic and hate sports. Or have long, elegant piano-playing fingers and prefer rapping instead. Bodies just get on with doing their jobs and helping you to do yours.

You shouldn't judge a book by its cover. (Unless you judged this book to be excellent by its cover, in which case you were one hundred per cent right). And that means you shouldn't judge your own body, either.

If you're not sure how to get started, you can try out lots of different hobbies and see what you enjoy and what you're good at. Don't assume that you won't be able to do something – just try it. And, remember, practice makes perfect. Your favourite footballer didn't climb out of their cot and start scoring hat-tricks. Your favourite singer wasn't born on the stage. They practised the skills that made them happy and they didn't let anything hold them back.

Love your body

Now we all agree our different bodies are brilliant, you'd think it would be easy to love them. But, sometimes we can look at other people and want what they have. You might be a beautiful singer but wish you had long legs so you could play basketball more easily. Or you might be a cracking cook but wish you could ace algebra instead. It's natural to compare yourself to the people around you. It can even be healthy if it spurs you on to practise more or study harder. But these feelings shouldn't ever make you feel bad about yourself.

Even if you feel confident, you might find it difficult to be surrounded by other people's insecurities. Have you heard people say they wish they were thinner, taller or prettier? That they'd like a smaller waist, longer legs, straighter hair or bigger muscles? It might make you start to look at yourself differently, too.

The best advice is to treat your body the way you treat your best friend. Be kind to your body, respect it and don't get too mad with it if it doesn't do what you want it to do. In the same way you can practise running or hockey to get better at them, you can practise being kind to yourself, too. You can say thank you to your body by looking after it and keeping it in good condition. **Eating healthily**, **getting enough sleep** and **moving regularly** are all good ways to show your body that you care about it.

Before you skip off to chapter three, remember:

THERE'S NO BODY ON EARTH LIKE YOURS!

Now finish this statement.

I promise to treat my body with respect. I love my body because:..
....
....
....
....
....
....
....

Keep calm and
BE KIND

In chapter two, we talked about what makes our bodies brilliant and we promised to treat our body like our best friend. But what about everyone else? It's possible that not everyone will read this. So, the big questions in this chapter are – how can we help the people around us to feel good about their bodies? How can we make sure other people treat ours with respect? Plus, you'll discover some modern life survival skills like how to deal with bullies and how to keep yourself safe online. And you'll find out your hidden superpower … you've got one, we promise!

Kindness is a bug

Kindness might seem small, maybe even insignificant, but when you're kind to a person it gives them fuzzy happy feelings. Before they know it, they've got the kindness bug and they're being kind to other people, too. Basically, by being nice to people you can make the world a better place. And that is super.

So, what's this got to do with our bodies? As we discussed in chapter two, our bodies help us to do some really cool stuff. But they can also be a source of insecurity – sometimes we wish they were different, then they go all puberty on us, and let's not forget the bogey-less celebs making us question what's real. So, with everyone walking around feeling a little bit body conscious, it's helpful to be kind and make other people feel good about themselves.

Here are some simple kind deeds you can try to make a big difference:

1. Lend your ears

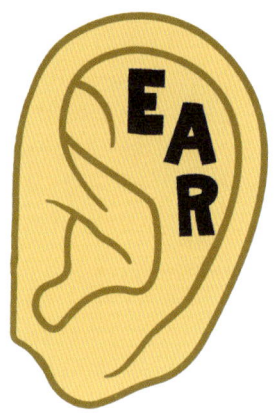

Your friends need an ear and you've got two! Let them talk about their worries. You don't have to offer advice, if you don't want to – a hug or just listening will do.

2. Don't be a sheep

Sheep may be friendly woolly beasts, but they move in herds and they don't think for themselves. You might find some sheep in your school. They're the ones who laugh when someone pokes fun at someone else. Don't let anyone pull the wool over your eyes – being mean to someone isn't fun. Ignore the laughter and – if you can – stand up for them. Remember: it's important to be your own person, following a crowd doesn't always make you cool.

3. Say nothing

You may have noticed that a friend has shot up a few inches and, as you're reading this book, you might think that they've started puberty. But the last thing they need is for you to point it out to them. Sometimes, it's best to say nothing – unless a friends asks to talk about it. Nothing, nadda, zip it.

Be a kind hero!

Do a kind deed every day this week and write about it here. What did you do? How did the person react and how did it make you feel?

Help to make dinner

Monday

....
....
....
....

Tuesday

....
....
....
....

Wednesday

....
....
....
....

Ask someone if they're okay if they look sad

Tell someone they look nice today

Thursday

....
....
....
....

Hold the door open for someone

Friday

....
....
....
....

Help a person carry their shopping

Saturday

....
....
....
....

Feed the birds

Sunday

....
....
....
....

Pick up litter

When people don't choose to be kind

Not everyone in the world spreads happiness. It's likely that at some point in your life you'll have encountered a bully. Bullies cause a stink. They parp unhappiness – great big guffs that get up people's noses and make them angry and upset. We often don't know why a bully behaves the way they do. But bullies are people, just like you or me. They have strengths, weaknesses, hopes and fears… If you're dealing with a bully, it helps to remember this.

Understanding bullying

In the last chapter, we agreed that every person is different. That means you probably won't get on with everyone you meet – and that's okay! We can live quite happily, side-by-side, letting other people get on with their lives while we get on with ours.

Unfortunately, bullies find it hard to leave other people alone. Bullies notice difference A LOT. They even fear it. So, bullies do whatever they can to make everyone else feel small. It doesn't matter if they're using physical violence or words, a bully is a person who deliberately hurts someone else to make themselves feel more powerful.

Bullying can be **physical** (like hitting or kicking), **emotional** (like name-calling or threats) or **cyber** (anything online). Every time a bully does something to make someone else feel little, they grow taller and get a feeling of power. Some bullies don't even realize they're doing it – they think it's funny to tease someone. But some bullies deliberately set out to make people sad. They don't care about other people's feelings.

Bullying can happen to anyone. It doesn't matter who you are or what you look like. The most important thing to remember is:

it's NEVER your fault.

It's the bully who has the problem, not you.

What to do if you're being bullied

WHEN PEOPLE STAND UP TO BULLIES, the bullies shrink.

(They don't actually shrink. But it would be cool if they did!)

You don't have to physically stand up to bullies or retaliate. But it's important to remember that you don't have to stay silent and let someone upset you.

This **TOP TIP** will help you be a bigger person than a bully:

If you or someone else is being bullied, don't just stand by and watch. Tell the bully to stop, or walk away and talk to an adult. That's the best way to take care of you, your friends and your body.

Try choosing a trusted person from this list:

your teacher

a school counsellor

a sibling

your mum or dad

a grandparent

a guardian

a friend

If you'd really rather not talk to someone you know, head to page 158 where you'll find telephone numbers for organisations with people who are trained to help you.

Some bullying myths – busted!

He or she is my friend so they can't bully me.

Unfortunately, bullying can happen in friendships and even in families, too. A good friend is kind and makes you feel good about yourself. You might have fallings out, but a true friend never sets out to make you feel bad or smaller than them.

I can't tease anyone anymore or I'll get called a bully.

Don't believe this one, either. No one's telling you not to have a laugh with your mates. You can have fun when there's no intention to hurt anyone and everyone knows the limits. But there's an invisible line and you can cross it without meaning to. So, if someone appears upset, apologize and don't tease them again. It's important never to make fun of anyone with the intention of humiliating them.

I didn't mean to be mean.

If you've unintentionally upset someone, it doesn't mean you're a bully. But it's important that you put it right. Apologize and ask the person what you can do to make them feel better and then give them the space they need to forgive you. Remember, words are easy to say but they can really hurt people. If you wouldn't like someone to say something to you, don't say it to anyone else.

He or she didn't hit me, so it can't be bullying.

Not true! Bullying can take many forms. It can happen verbally or physically, face-to-face or online. If someone repeatedly hurts another person to make themselves feel more powerful then they're bullying that person.

Remember to choose kind

Just as no one should ever try to bully you, you should never bully or join in bullying other people. It's much cooler to choose to be kind. If you're not sure, remember, it's never okay to pick on someone because they are different to you or come from a different culture or background. Learning to accept other people is an important part of growing up.

Between friends

Being friends with someone is hard. It doesn't matter how much you like your friends, you're bound to fall out sometimes. You might row and say hurtful things in the heat of the moment. But the difference between rowing and bullying is that you're both still equal. One person isn't always putting the other person down to make themselves feel powerful.

If you feel your friend is always being mean and upsetting you then it might be better for you to end the friendship. There's lots more advice about this in chapter six. For now, remember no one should make you feel sad, especially your mates. And while friends don't grow on trees (that would be weird), there are lots of amazing, unique people out there waiting to meet you.

A whole new world

In the olden days, people didn't have computers or smart phones. Then along came technology and everything changed... Nowadays, the world is always in your pocket and it's noisy. You can:

video call your friends, turn yourself into a puppy, listen to music, research homework, learn to play the guitar and watch random videos of cats falling off stuff

– ALL AT THE SAME TIME!

The Internet is amazing, but it's also huge. Think of it like a city. If you were going into the city without your mum and dad, they'd want to know that you were being streetwise and staying safe.

The Internet is bigger than any city and it's full of strangers. The fact it exists in a smartphone or computer doesn't make it any less real.

Surf safely

It's important to remember that when you're surfing online you've got an audience, but you can't see them. These people are like sea creatures beneath the ocean. Most of them are harmless fish but you don't know if there's a shark lurking.

When you post information online, it can make it easier for strangers to find out about you. But if you keep your information private, it keeps the sharks at bay.

Remember to be web wise!

Here are some top tips to help you surf safely and have fun at the same time.

- If you do go online, it's important to ask permission and let your mum, dad or guardian know. The more honest and open you are with them, the more likely they are to trust you to use the Internet.

- **If something makes you feel uncomfortable tell a grown-up straight away.**

- Keep your full name, address and phone number private.

- **Ask a grown-up to help you create your passwords.**

- If you wouldn't do it face-to-face, don't do it online. That goes for talking to strangers or being unpleasant to friends.

- **Remember, once you write it you can't delete it. ANYONE can read it, including your mum and dad, uncle and aunt and even future employers.**

- Don't accept gifts from strangers – that includes mail attachments or photos. If you don't know who sent it, don't open it.

Cyberbullying is real

Technology has changed the world. It's amazing to be able to connect with family and friends wherever you are. But it has also given bullies more tools to bully people with. Cyberbullying is any form of bullying that is carried out through the use of electronic devices, such as computers, laptops, smartphones, tablets or gaming consoles. And it's every bit as real as bullying that happens face-to-face.

What to do if you're being bullied online

If you're being cyberbullied, it can make you feel upset and scared, even though it doesn't physically hurt you. It can be difficult to know what to do about it because getting access to the Internet or a mobile phone is so easy and messages and information can be sent out so quickly. If it happens to you, don't be tempted to respond to any of the nasty comments. That is just what the bully wants you to do. Instead, follow these simple steps:

TELL a grown-up

BLOCK the person so they can't bully again

REPORT the bullying to the social media platform it was carried out on

www.net-aware.org.uk has details on how to block and report users for all the major social media apps.

Be your own superhero

In this chapter, we've been helping other people to feel good about their bodies – you get a big gold star for all of those kind deeds you did. And we've been learning how to make sure other people treat us and our bodies with respect. If you think this last one is more difficult, you're right! It's easier to change our own behaviour than that of the people around us. So, here's a little secret. We all have a secret superpower that can protect our body…

That superpower is being kind to yourself.

When we respect ourselves, we feel confident. And when we feel confident, without even meaning to, we make ourselves bigger. That's not just a metaphor. We hold ourselves upright, we walk taller, we look people in the eye. And that makes us a more difficult target for bullies.

Even if a bully tries to make us feel small, we know that we and our body deserve better. We act quickly and we tell someone about it. We stop a bully in their tracks.

Remember how you wrote down what you love about your body at the end of the last chapter? Turn back to page 29 and read it again now. Then give yourself a hug and remember that YOU deserve to be treated with respect.

Love your world

After reading this chapter, you might think that the world is full of people who want to hurt each other. But that's not true. Most people are friendly and kind. So, take the advice from this chapter, slip it in your back pocket and go and enjoy yourself.

Before you dash off, finish this statement.

I promise to be kind. I will make other people feel body positive by:

FASTER, BRAVER, STRONGER

Yes, YOU CAN!

You started this journey by celebrating everything that's brilliant about your body, then you learned how to spread kindness and use your superpower (being kind to yourself) to make other people treat you with respect. Now you've reached the chapter where you can give something back to your body. One of the best ways to say thank you is by giving your body a present... Nope, not flowers, or chocolate, or even A GREAT BIG FLUFFY TEDDY THAT SAYS YOUR NAME WHEN YOU SQUEEZE IT! What bodies love more than anything else is moving. Here's why...

You like to move it, move it

Exercise makes you feel good on the inside and out. Let's prove it. Put on your favourite song and dance like no one's watching. Sing, jump, fling your arms around, really throw some shapes. How do you feel? A bit out of breath, maybe. But it's likely you're grinning from ear to ear. That's thanks to endorphins.

Endorph-WHAT?

Endorphins is the big name for the hormones your body releases when you exercise. Best of all, they make you feel great. So great, in fact, scientists say exercise can help you feel happy when you've been blue. Plus, here's the biggie – exercise makes you feel body confident.

And it's FREE!

Exercise is just moving

Sometimes, it can feel like exercise is this thing other people love to do. It's all very well if you've always loved football, if you're a natural on a tennis court or if you always score the winning goal in hockey. But what if you feel happier curled up with a good book? If you'd much rather sit in English than do PE? If you break out in a sweat at the thought of running a mile?

The good news is exercise just means moving. There's no difference between running on a racetrack and running around a playground – except that one feels like exercise and the other is just playtime! The best plan is to figure out what you enjoy doing – and who with – and turn that into your own special way to exercise.

Hockey or hula-hooping, cycling or street dancing, what's your ideal way to get moving? Take this quiz to find out!

How would your friends describe you?
- a) chilled
- b) a good laugh
- c) a team player

You've got a spare hour, do you:
- a) curl up with a book
- b) call a mate to chat
- c) compete with your friends in a computer game

What's your favourite subject?
- a) English
- b) Drama
- c) PE

You find a football, do you:
- a) ignore it
- b) head it
- c) get your friends together for a game

Which Olympic sport do you enjoy watching?
- a) diving
- b) beach volleyball
- c) tennis

What's your ideal birthday party?
- a) the cinema
- b) a disco
- c) bowling

Turn the page to discover your answer!

Mostly As: you're a cool mover

Low impact exercise will suit your chilled personality. If you'd rather work out alone, try cycling, golf or swimming. Yoga and Pilates are great if you want to join a class and exercise with other people. Or try signing up to a martial arts course to help you feel more powerful and confident.

Mostly Bs: you're fun-loving

You love to enjoy life so choose playful activities like dancing, skipping or hula-hooping. You could even set up an assault course in your garden, or run, swim or cycle with a friend to make you feel less like you're exercising and more like you're just having fun.

Mostly Cs: you're a team player

You love nothing more than playing group games, so the sport world is your oyster! Football, hockey, tennis, basketball, street dancing and rugby all have teammates plus strategies to keep your brain moving as well as your body.

Mix it up

The ideal way to exercise is to make your body move in lots of different ways. If you love low impact sports like walking and swimming then push yourself to try jogging or trampolining. Or, if you love kicking a ball around, slow down and learn yoga. You might surprise yourself and find something new that you love. Remember, you can always practise harder and push yourself to get better at the sport you love. And, every time you do, your body will love you a little bit more.

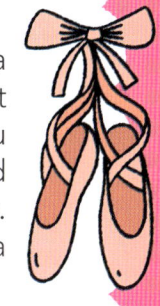

There's a sport for everyone

Still not inspired? Pick something from this list!

- AQUA AEROBICS
- UNICYCLING
- HAVING A DANCE OFF
- CLIMBING A TREE
- HORSE RIDING
- ARCHERY
- KITE FLYING
- TABLE TENNIS
- ULTIMATE FRISBEE
- SURFING
- KAYAKING
- VOLLEYBALL
- BADMINTON
- BREAKDANCING
- CHEERLEADING
- WELLY TOSSING
- BALLET
- PLAYING TAG
- ICE SKATING
- HURDLING

Not today, thanks!

The weird thing about exercise is that even though our bodies love it, sometimes it's hard to get them moving. The toughest part about exercising is getting started, but it's easy if you know how…

• Just do it!

The best tip is to stop thinking and start doing. If you're lying down, wiggle your fingers and your toes to wake yourself up. Sit up and put on your trainers. Turn off the TV and put on some motivational music instead. Tell yourself you CAN do it. Let your body take over and do what it loves best.

• Dangle a carrot

Once upon a time, people travelled by horse and they dangled a carrot in front of the horse to get it to move. (Horses *really* like carrots). You can try combining moving with something you love to make it more fun. Jog while listening to an audiobook, cycle on a stationary bike while watching your favourite TV series or dance whenever you listen to your favourite album. Soon, you'll want to exercise every day.

- **Exercise, sleep, repeat**

How often do you think, *'I should clean my teeth'* or *'I can't be bothered to eat my breakfast?'* Not very often. We do these daily tasks at the same time every day without giving them a moment's thought. If you can make exercise as much a part of your daily routine as putting on your pyjamas then it'll become something you do without thinking. Walk or scoot to school, join a Monday night sports club or go for a jog every Saturday morning – you'll soon find yourself exercising without thinking about it.

- **Think positive**

You can create a mental mountain when you think of exercise as a chore. If exercise is something you enjoy, you're more likely to want to do it. Say,

'I want to do this!'

instead of *'I've got to!'* Your thoughts have power over your actions so turn them into motivation instead of hurdles.

The great news is, the more you exercise, the easier it is to remember that your body loves it and the more you want to do it. So, what are you waiting for? Get moving!

Silence the gremlins

Do you think, **'I can't do sport – I'm rubbish at it! If people see me exercise, they'll think I look stupid.'** How about, **'I couldn't hit the ball in PE – it was just too embarrassing.'** Or **'I'll never play as well as that person so there's no point in trying.'**

We agreed in chapter two that every body is unique, so it makes sense that we can't all be good at everything. But, with hard work and practice, you can train your body to get better at different skills. The trick is not to give yourself a hard time. If there's a sport you'd love to be better at – practise with a family member or friend, but don't expect miracles to happen overnight. And try other activities, too. You may not have the hand-eye coordination for baseball but what about the drive and the build to be a swimmer, a runner or a cyclist? Everybody is good at something – and that's a fact.

Be inspired

If you're finding that hard to believe, read Harry's story...

> Harry loved football and he practised hard. When he was six, he played at a local club and then, when he was eight, he was spotted by Arsenal.

> But within a year, Arsenal let him go. Harry went back to being a regular kid who liked football. So, what did he do next?

Did Harry give up football because he'd just been rejected and it was hard and embarrassing? Or did he keep playing football because he loved it and wanted to get better, then end up playing for England and scoring six goals in the 2018 World Cup?

Yep, that's right. We're talking about English football champ, Harry Kane. He could have given up his dream, but he kept playing and practising and then, when he was 11, he was spotted by Tottenham. After that, every time Harry played Arsenal, he went out and was determined to beat the team who had dropped him. He said, 'Looking back on it now, it was probably the best thing that ever happened to me, because it gave me a drive that wasn't there before.'

Now, of course, Harry 'Hurri-kane' is a national hero, but his career has been full of setbacks and he's kept fighting every step of the way. He says, 'Life never hands it to you, does it? You've got to grab it.'

And if Harry hasn't convinced you, maybe one of these amazing athletes will…

'Luck has nothing to do with it, because I have spent many, many hours, countless hours, on the court working for my one moment in time, not knowing when it would come.'

World tennis champion Serena Williams

'When you fail, you learn a lot about yourself and come back stronger. Life need not have limits.'

Team GB Paralympic marathon runner Richard Whitehead

'I've failed over and over again in my life. And that is why I succeed.'

Basketball legend Michael Jordan

'It's kind of crazy to me that I'm now an Olympian and went from being told that I couldn't even do this sport at one point.'

US women's wrestler Adeline Gray

Now, before you bust a move, you know what to do – finish the sentence!

I CAN do it! My new weekly exercise will be:..........................

....

....

....

....

....

....

YOU GOTTA NOURISH TO FLOURISH

Take a bite OUT OF life!

Here we are sprinting into chapter five ... surely it must be time for a snack? Yes! This chapter is all about food. Get ready to discover how to eat with your mind and body, discover the super squad that will make your body feel amazing and find out why we love junk food so much. Oh, and you'll meet your inner caveperson – which is cool!

The first rule of food is there are no rules!

People are always saying you should or shouldn't eat certain foods. One minute they're banning bread, and then bread's okay but they're not eating fat. The fact is we need fat – it oils our joints and keeps our brains healthy. And we need carbs like bread – they give us the energy to run around. It is important to keep your body healthy, but it doesn't need to be complicated. Just enjoy eating lots of different types of food. Just listen to your body and enjoy eating lots of different types of food.

This food is super!

We've agreed we need to be kind to our bodies to say thank you for the amazing things they do for us. And what do our bodies need to give them the fuel to move? You guessed it – food! Include these foods in your diet to give your mind and body superpowers!

Jacket potato
Super ingredients: fibre and B-vitamins
Superpowers: helps your immune system, keeps you fuller for longer and makes you feel ready for anything!
Alternatives: wholegrain bread and pasta

Salmon
Super ingredients: protein, amino acids, omega-3
Superpowers: helps you to grow and helps to protect your brain
Alternatives: oily fish (like sardines, trout and mackerel) nuts, eggs for protein and omega-3. Lean meat, poultry and soy products are also good sources of protein

Milk

Super ingredients: calcium, omega-3

Superpowers: helps your body to build strong bones, teeth and muscles, plus healthy hair and skin and helps you to fight off colds and bugs

Alternatives: yoghurt, cheese, calcium-fortified vegan alternatives

Lentils

Super ingredients: iron, protein, fibre, vitamins and minerals

Superpowers: help you to grow and make you feel ready for anything!

Alternatives: for protein and omega-3, try oily fish, nuts or eggs

These foods are a good source of protein: lean meat, poultry and soy products

Ask your mum or dad if you can add some of these super foods to your weekly shopping list.

The friendly fats

There are different kinds of fats and while some aren't that healthy, others are super important as they keep us moving. Aim to eat nuts (as long as you're not allergic), seeds, fish and oils like olive oil to keep yourself in tip-top shape!

Have your cake and eat it

Once you've got these super foods in your life, you can carve up your diet into portions and give yourself treats, too. To keep your brilliant body happy, aim to eat this way every day:

Five portions of fruit and veg – try apples, oranges, berries, star fruits (trust me, they're real) tomatoes, carrots, broccoli, sweetcorn, spinach, bananas, dragon fruit (yep), whatever takes your fancy.

Starchy foods – such as potatoes, bread, rice and pasta. Choose wholemeal to keep you fuller for longer.

Proteins – fill up on fish, lean meat, eggs, lentils, beans and nuts and seeds.

Dairy and alternatives – don't miss out milk, yoghurt and cheese, which contain essential fats.

Treats – eat small amounts of crisps, chocolate and sweets.

EATWELL GUIDE

- WATER — 6-8 A DAY
- STARCHY FOODS
- UNSATURATED OILS
- DAIRY AND ALTERNATIVES
- PROTEINS
- TREATS
- FRUIT AND VEG

Different Diets

Sometimes, people choose to eat an alternative diet. Two diets you might have heard of are vegetarianism and veganism. Vegetarians choose not to eat meat. But they do eat animal products like milk and eggs. People who are vegan choose to eat a purely plant-based diet. That means they don't eat any animal products at all. People who are vegan usually choose to be because they don't like the idea of eating animals or because they want to do something positive for the planet.

If you'd like to try vegetarianism or veganism, then the most important thing is to make sure that you are getting all the nutrition you need to stay fit and healthy, especially while you are growing. If you decide you'd like to choose a vegan diet, talk to your mum or dad to help you find out what you should be eating to ensure you get all the essentials your body needs.

Just add water

Your body needs water to work properly and to avoid dehydration. But how much is enough? The general advice is six to eight glasses a day, but you'll need more if you've been exercising or sweating a lot. Basically, your body loses water throughout the day and it's up to you to put it back in. If you find water boring and eight glasses sounds like a lot, try making it taste more exciting by adding a splash of fruit juice or even try fruit tea. But don't drink too many drinks that have lots of sugar in them, like fizzy drinks, undiluted juice and even smoothies. (Some fizzy drinks contain over 10 g of sugar per 100 ml.) It might be hard to believe that a drink can have that much sugar in. But these drinks are one of the reasons lots of people are becoming overweight.

Easy ways to make your meals super

The more colours you eat, the more health benefits you get so try to use fruit and vegetables to make your plate look like a rainbow.

Add a chopped banana or berries to your morning wholegrain cereal or porridge.

Add some cucumber, lettuce, tomato or even carrot to your sandwiches.

Try adding peas, carrots or spring onions into mashed potatoes.

Sprinkle some extra veg on to your pizza like sweetcorn, pepper and mushrooms.

Eat with the seasons to mix up your diet. Berries in the summer, pumpkin in the autumn. It's the way our great great great (great great) grandparents used to eat.

Food is your friend

Sometimes, you might hear people feeling bad about eating too much or the wrong things, but YOU know food is really important. It helps your body to grow and move. To understand why food can make people feel this way, it's good to understand why we eat what we eat.

To zoom from home to school, a car and a person need fuel. For a car, that fuel is usually petrol. For a person, that fuel is food. With cars, in goes the fuel and off the car goes. Cars don't guzzle fuel because they're bored or because they had a row with a friend, because they aced a test or they're watching a movie… But humans consume food for all of these reasons and many, many more.

Comfort Food

Let's whizz back in time to when we were tiny babies. When we cried, we were given food (aka milk). That food made us feel loved and safe. Right from birth, we had an emotional connection to what we ate. As we get older, there are lots of ways that we can feel comfort. Yes, a chocolate cake can tell us that someone loves us. But, so can a card, a friendly message or even a smile. We can talk, feel listened to and ask for a hug. There are lots of ways to feel better if you're having a bad day.

Sweet treats

According to research, when we're told to treat ourselves, most of us reach for food. Nine times out of ten, that treat contains sugar, salt or fat (sometimes all three – hello, salted caramel ice cream). There's a reason for this – these foods make us feel good. Eating small amounts of them is okay but, in large quantities, these foods are bad for our health. There are lots of other fun ways to treat yourself. Buying a new magazine, giving yourself a night off homework or a nice hot bubble bath will all make you feel great.

Hello, cavepeople

If you're thinking, **'Whoa there! It's almost like we can't help craving junk food,'** – you'd be right! It's time to whizz a lot further back in time to meet our inner cavepeople.

A very, very long time ago, shortly after we evolved from apes, humans roamed the land eating whatever they could lay their hands on. A berry here, some roots there. Maybe a juicy grub as a treat. We were always moving in search of food. Believe it or not, there were no packets of crisps growing on trees. Cavepeople couldn't wolf down a bar of chocolate while lying down playing with their new iRock. Salt, sugar and fat were rare, but very useful. Salt helped the body to hold on to water – it basically turned us into camels. Sugar provided a quick burst of energy, which was essential if a sabre-toothed tiger was heading our way. Fat was stored by our bodies for when food was short. That meant, in cave dwelling times, we experienced a rush of pleasure whenever we ate these foods – and that's still a part of our brains today.

Nowadays, in our developed world, most people have enough food and water. We sit down A LOT more than cavepeople did and there are NO sabre-toothed tigers lurking on the journey to the shop (phew!). Plus, fat, sugar and salt are EVERYWHERE.

Even though we don't need to eat them every day, our caveperson instincts make it really hard to resist a juicy cheeseburger or a squidgy brownie – especially when they're shouting at us from posters, the television and supermarket shelves.

You don't have to ban the burgers

So, just how bad is it to eat these foods? Most people consume too much salt, which can lead to high blood pressure and other serious diseases. Meanwhile, too much sugar and fat are the leading causes of being very overweight (obese). More than six in ten adults in the UK are obese and that's leading to serious health risks.

No one's saying you can never eat a burger, but you should eat a balanced diet that includes a mix of healthy foods and treats. Try the experiment on the next page to encourage you to enjoy lots of different types of foods…

Eat with your mind and body

Over the next week, eat a food from each group on this list and record what it's like. Eat it slowly, take your time to really taste it. Is it salty or sweet? Maybe spicy or bitter? What does it feel like to chew? Is it hot or cold? Then be really, really honest with yourself – how much do you enjoy it? Finally, write how you feel afterwards – full, still hungry, happy, energized, tired, bloated – it's your body, so listen to what it's telling you.

chocolate – milk, white or dark	tofu or chicken
cheese (or non-dairy cheese)	wholewheat bread or cereal
strawberry, peach or blueberry	carrot, sweetcorn or peas
lemon or lime	crisps – any flavour you like
potato – boiled, baked or mashed	white bread or pasta

Monday

Food:

Notes:

Tuesday

Food:

Notes:

Wednesday

Food:

Notes:

Thursday

Food:

Notes:

Friday

Food:

Notes:

Saturday

Food:

Notes:

Sunday

Food:

Notes:

At the end of the week, look back and see what surprised you. I bet you enjoyed some foods far more than you thought you would. And maybe some of the ones you thought you loved didn't quite stand up to the test. The important thing is to enjoy eating these foods and to discover some new favourites that you might not have tried before.

I'm on a seafood diet. I see food and I eat it

Dad joke alert! But do you know why it's funny? Because, like all good jokes, it's true… Imagine there's a chocolate bar in front of you. You're trying to concentrate on something really fun but the chocolate bar is talking to you. It's saying, **'Hey you!'** And, if you ignore it, it starts shouting: **'EAT ME! I'M DELICIOUS!'** And if you ignore it, still, it starts using mind sorcery and before you know it your mouth's watering and you can taste the chocolate and you know you're going to eat it so you might as well put it in your mouth right now!

It's true, right? Now, go and find a handful of grapes, an apple, some carrot sticks – whatever you've got lurking in your kitchen.

Now, put the healthy food close by, where you can see it. Maybe hold it in your hand. And it's likely the same thing will happen. You won't be able to help eating it. Which just goes to prove, you can make yourself want healthy food – you've just got to surround yourself with it every day.

Best practices for eating

It's not just what you eat that matters – but how you eat it. Be a meal changer and try to encourage all of your family to eat like this:

Don't skip breakfast. Skipping meals means you miss out on nutrients and you're more likely to reach for an unhealthy muffin or biscuit when you get peckish.

Try different foods. People are unique and we all like different things. But it's fun to try new and exciting foods to get your taste buds grooving.

Help your parents or guardian to make meals. If you're helping to make the food you can help choose what's on the menu. Why not make homemade fish fingers or veggie-packed pizzas?

Food for thought

Sometimes, a person's relationship with food can become difficult and they can develop what is known as an eating disorder. An eating disorder can involve eating too much or too little or becoming worried about your body weight or shape.

Some **signs of an eating disorder** can include:

- eating very little food or only low-calorie food
- exercising too much
- losing or gaining a lot of weight
- avoiding places where people eat together

If you're worried that you or anyone you know could be developing an eating disorder, it's important to get help. Talk to a trusted adult – it doesn't have to be your mum or dad, it could be a teacher, an aunt, or even a friend's mum or dad. If you really feel you can't talk to someone you know, look on page 158 for details of organisations that can help. The sooner you can get help the better. Remember, our bodies can't function without the right amount of food to keep us healthy and strong.

Before you skip off to eat an apple, finish this sentence.

My body deserves the best food. I'm going to fill up on healthy:..

....

....

....

....

....

....

BE WHO YOU ARE & SAY WHAT YOU FEEL. BECAUSE THOSE WHO mind DON'T matter & THOSE WHO Matter DON'T MIND.

DR SEUSS

Squad goals

By now, you love your brilliant body and you're giving yourself the exercise and food you need to shine inside and out. Plus, you're treating others with respect and expecting them to do the same in return. You're an all-round amazing human and who knows that better than anyone? Your friends!

But how easily does this awesome YOU fit in with your friendship group? And how much do the people around you affect your decisions? This chapter is all about how to stay true to yourself, while being an amazing friend.

Your squad

Friends are special and it's likely thinking about them is making you grin. You know each other better than any other person in the world. You've shared the BEST times – and you make each other laugh. You've probably scribbled notes to each other in maths or said the same thing at the same time and it was just so funny! Sometimes you feel like no one gets you the same way your best mate does. You know who those extra special people in your life are. They're your right arm and your left leg, the sunshine on a rainy day …

the cherry on your cake.

You're the best!

Fill in lots of fun facts about your best friends (if you have loads of friends, copy the questions on to a fresh piece of paper).

My friend's name: ....

Age: ....

How we met: ....

....

They're the cherry on the cake because: ....

....

We LOVE doing this together: ....

....

The BIGGEST difference between us is: ....

....

The funniest thing we did was: ....

....

If I was down, this friend would say: ....

....

They make me feel: ....

....

....

....

Opposites attract

The chances are, when you filled in these facts, you realized you and your friends are not the same. You may have stuff in common but, as we know, everybody is different. It's likely these differences are what make your friendship special. Friends don't have to be identical, they just have to work together – like bacon and eggs or cookies and milk. Yum! If one of you plays the drums and the other plays the guitar, what a great match!

YOU-NIQUE

When people hang out a lot they start to say the same things, share 'in' jokes and even finish each other's sentences. That's a lot of fun. But, sometimes, when you like someone, you can start acting so much like them that you lose sight of who you really are. It might start with buying the same top or choosing the same chocolate bar, and end up with saying one thing when you think the opposite. Your friend will still like you if you don't share their point of view, and, if you slowly turn into your friend, you'll lose the magic combination that made your friendship special in the first place.

Stay true to YOU

Then there are the times when friends try to get you to behave in a way that isn't you. They might want you to skip lunch and eat chocolate instead, to talk in class when you're trying to listen or to make fun of another person when you know it's not kind. You might think, **'I like my friend and I want to make them happy. But I won't feel happy if I do this thing.'** Remember: a friend should NEVER put you in a situation where you are uncomfortable. Friends should respect each other.

How to say no

This two-letter word has the power to help you always be YOU. Practise saying it in the mirror. Be firm, smile, shake your head. And don't feel like you need to make an excuse.

No!

No, thank you.

That's not for me, thanks.

I'd rather not.

I'll pass.

Say it in the way that feels the most comfortable to you, and say it whenever and wherever you want to.

Of course, you can say YES, too. **'Yes, I'd like to play,' 'Yes, let's get a second helping,' 'Yes, I'd love to run down the street singing Ed Sheeran at the top of my voice!'**

Saying NO doesn't make you boring. It says, **'I'm strong, I know my own mind, and I'm comfortable with who I am.'**

Three's the magic number

How many friends did you write about? One, maybe two or even more? It's great having one really close best friend, and sometimes that might feel like all you need. But there are benefits to having lots of close mates that you might not have thought of.

When you and a mate fall out
If you have just one friend, you're going to feel pretty lonely until you make up. But if you've got more than one, you'll still have a good friend to hang out with. They might even help you to make up with your other friend quicker.

When you fancy doing something different

Remember, everybody is different. So, if you have a big friendship group, you'll have someone to hang out with whatever your mood. The cinema, shopping, playing tennis, making slime – the more friends you have, the more fun things you can do.

When you need a helping hand

Sometimes you need to chat, other times you need someone to make you laugh, and then there are the times when you need advice. If you've got lots of friends you'll have different people to help you through the tricky times.

Friendship wobbles

Friendships bring so much happiness into our lives, but they can bring confusion and even insecurity, too. Sometimes, we can overthink our friendships and imagine things that aren't there. We might feel left out or worry that our friends have more fun without us. The problem is, once we start thinking these things, we start to act differently. We might be less likely to pick up the phone or to invite a friend over to our house. We imagine if they cared about us, they'd message first. We can create a problem where there wasn't one before.

If you find yourself feeling like this, try to talk to someone about how you feel. If you don't feel able to talk to your friends, then try someone else you trust, like a parent, sibling or even a teacher. They'll help you to talk out your feelings and work out if there's any truth in them. If your friends are leaving you out, they might not mean to be and they can't fix the problem if they don't know how you feel.

Friendship fixes

Friendships hit bumpy patches, but that doesn't mean you're going to lose your best mate. In fact, arguing can actually make a friendship stronger – it's better to get your feelings out and move on from a disagreement than to let bad feelings grow inside you. But it can feel horrible to fall out with your best friend. Fortunately, there are several ways to fix a friendship problem:

> Cool down: arguing is okay, but the best way to get your feelings out is to explain how you feel. And that means you need a cool, rational head.

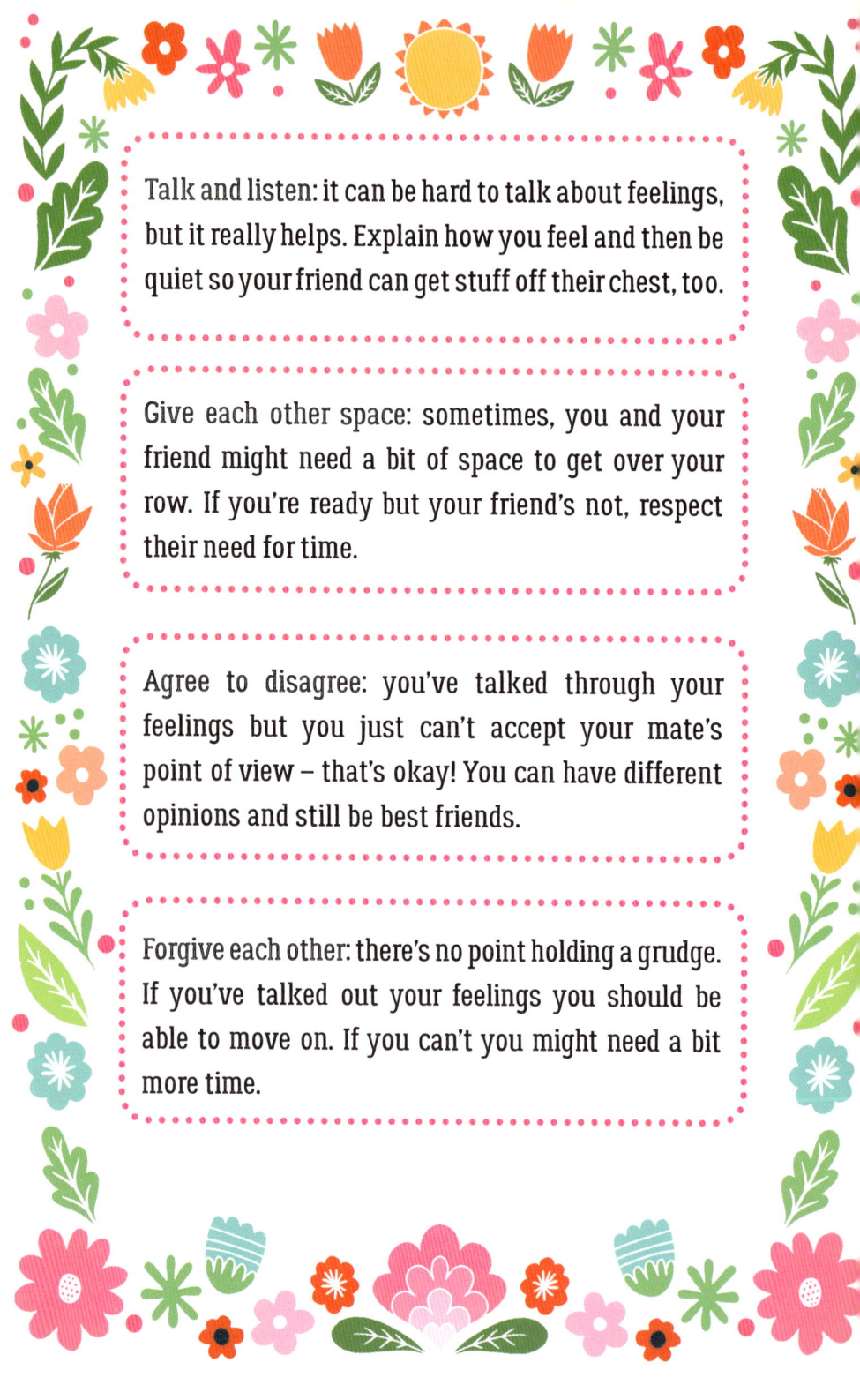

Talk and listen: it can be hard to talk about feelings, but it really helps. Explain how you feel and then be quiet so your friend can get stuff off their chest, too.

Give each other space: sometimes, you and your friend might need a bit of space to get over your row. If you're ready but your friend's not, respect their need for time.

Agree to disagree: you've talked through your feelings but you just can't accept your mate's point of view – that's okay! You can have different opinions and still be best friends.

Forgive each other: there's no point holding a grudge. If you've talked out your feelings you should be able to move on. If you can't you might need a bit more time.

Friends are forever?

Think back to when you met your best friends. Maybe it was when you started school and you bonded over a shared love of squishies. Or did you meet at a club, like acting or dancing, and discover you had the same heroes? Perhaps, you met at playschool and babbled about milk and smelly nappies or whatever babies chat about. Something made you pick out your friends as the special people in your life. And it's likely you still have lots in common to chat, giggle and moan about.

But people grow and change all of the time. In fact, you're at a time in your life when people change the most. (Hello, puberty!) Even a person you met last year might suddenly start to hate hockey although though they're captain of the team. They might say fart jokes are childish when we all know they are – and always will be – hilarious. Reading this book might have made you look at life a little differently. Maybe you're more likely to talk to new people or are trying new things. If you and your friends are growing and changing in the same direction, that's great – and very special. You don't have to be exactly the same, remember. You just need to be on the same wavelength.

But sometimes, friends reach a fork in the road and its okay if you don't want to travel in the same direction. It could make you happier to go your own way.

IS IT THE END OF THE ROAD?

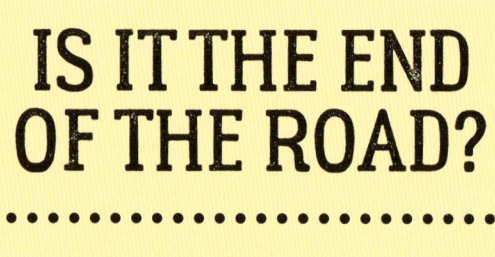

If you answer yes to any of these questions, your friendship might be reaching the end of its natural life cycle.

- You and your friend always want to do very different things.
- You don't agree with your friend's opinions.
- You feel like you just don't get your friend any more or they don't get you.
- You find it much harder to chat to your friend than you used to.
- When you fall out, you can't get over it – even when you try to talk to each other about it.
- You feel like your friend doesn't respect you any more.
- You generally feel unhappy when you've spent time together.

This might make you feel sad, and that's okay. The best advice is to surround yourself with people who make you feel good. These people will become the new important friends in your life. But remember to be kind. Your friend might not have realized yet that your lives are moving in different directions.

There are new best friends everywhere

When you've got great friends, it's easy to close your eyes to other people around you. But new special people are waiting to be discovered all of the time! Look out for them when you join a new club or in the school playground. If there's been a big change in your life, like moving schools, you'll be surrounded by new people. If you feel worried about talking to them, remember that your best friends were strangers once.

The best way to make new friends is to be open to meeting new people. Try introducing yourself with a smile. Everyone loves to talk about the things they like – try asking about their favourite singer or subject at school. And remember to listen to what they've got to say. If you like their smile, share their hobbies or love their opinions, be brave and invite them to hang out at your house. You never know where this new friendship might lead.

Now finish this sentence.

I promise to always be true to ME. The friends who get me make me feel: ....

....
....
....
....
....
....

PERFECT AT BEING YOU

Keeping it real

How real is the world you live in? That might seem like an odd question. But we've talked about the online world and how to use it safely. And we've mentioned that perfect pictures of celebrities aren't what they seem. In this chapter, we're going to give you the special power of being able to see the truth – even when what you're looking at isn't real. Think of life as being like a magic show and we're going to show you how the smoke and mirrors work. It's something even grown-ups struggle with. But, after reading this chapter, you're going to be amazing at it. Just wait and see…

Who can you be real with?

Your best friends and your family are the people who make you feel the most like you. You never feel like you have to act differently around them, or pretend to be someone you're not. You're totally comfortable with who you are.

Now, let's imagine you're with a group of people from school who you don't know as well. Do you behave differently? Are you more worried about how you appear, or aware of how you sound? On the outside, you're smiling and talking but inside you're thinking about what to say. People should like you for who you really are, but sometimes we fall into the trap of trying to put on our 'best self'. This is normal. Even though you might be out of your comfort zone, remember to be yourself, because that's what matters.

Social ME-dia

You've probably heard of social media sites and you might be thinking about using them in the future. You can be connected to hundreds and hundreds of people online – and you might not know all of them. Remember the way you feel when you meet new people and want to present your best self? Social media makes some people behave like that all of the time. They make themselves look and sound amazing.

Protect your image

If you do decide to put yourself on social media one day, remember it's important to protect your identity. Once your photos are on the web you can't control who sees them. Only put photos online that you'd be happy to show to your grandma.

And if you wouldn't be happy to show any photograph to a person in the street, do you really want to be putting them online?

My perfect life

We hang out with people online, too, and that gives us a lot more time to edit ourselves. In fact, we do it without even thinking. You might be using group-messaging apps to speak to your friends while sitting in your pyjamas, picking your nose (and even eating it) and they will never know. You can write a message and change it to make it funnier, write an opinion then delete it without pressing send, and take a photo – then a better one, which is the one you end up sending. You're chatting to the people you feel the most REAL with but you still end up trying to give them the 'best' version of you.

Keep it real...

A typical social media newsfeed is full of people shouting,

'Look at ME!'

It might look something like this:

Having the most amazing holiday ever! Wish you were here? LOL

Just ran 10 miles and not even tired!

Love these guys to the moon and back. BEST FRIENDS FOREVER

Never mind that these best friends just had a massive row, or the 'runner' walked a mile and put on make-up before taking the photo. Who wouldn't love to be lying on a beach? But, next week, the person on the beach will be trudging to school in the rain and they won't post a photo then. Social media is like a shop window. People put the best bits of their life on display, and they hide all of the bits that they don't want you to see in the back of a cupboard.

You might wonder why people bother. But it's a vicious circle. When people put their best self out there, other people feel like they have to compete and make their own lives look amazing.

So, what's the harm if everyone is doing it? The problem is, if we see amazingly positive stories or altered images all the time, we tend to forget what's real. We start to think we're the only person in the world not lying on a sunny beach. We look at our red, sweaty face after exercising and wonder why it doesn't look like the perfect faces in the photos. We have a row with our friends and feel like it's just us who can't get along with people.

In the playground, we see people for who they really are. We see them row, sweat, blush and stumble over their words. Online, we often don't see anything 'real' or 'human'. We've talked about keeping you and your body safe by being web wise. But if you believe what you see, social media can also mess with your mind.

TO BE SOCIAL MEDIA SMART YOU NEED TO REMEMBER:

people put their 'best self' online

it's not real

no one's life is perfect

The fame game

Look around you next time you're on the train or on a bus. We're surrounded by people who look, sound and think differently. It's what makes every person special. Now look around again. How many of those people are looking at each other and how many have their nose glued to their phone? We might even spend more time looking at famous people in apps, magazines, television programmes, films and adverts than we do looking at real people. And how many different body shapes, races or cultures are in those pictures? You guessed it – not many.

Somebody decides who we're going to look at and how those people should appear. They edit the world. And, if we're not careful, they can get into our heads. When you see these images all the time, you can start to think perfect-looking celebrities are normal. And if you can't see anyone who looks like you, you might start to think you're the one who needs to change. That's not fair. Yet this happens every single day.

Picture perfect

Most of the images you're looking at aren't even real. Here's why we will NEVER look like pictures of celebrities…

Teams of hair and make-up artists spend hours covering spots, making eyes pop and gluing hair so the model or celebrity looks as perfect as possible. Imagine hiring a hair or make-up artist to come to your bedroom at 5 am every morning before school!

Special lighting is used to make skin look like it glows and to make eyes, muscles and cheekbones really stand out.

Then the photos are edited to make the already perfect person look EVEN MORE PERFECT! Special tools remove marks, make eyes bigger, make waists smaller and make legs look longer... NO ONE could ever look like this in real life.

Of course, famous people don't look like that day-to-day. We just don't see that very often. Sometimes a newspaper will show you a picture of a celeb 'dressed down' and be a bit nasty about it – they'll draw circles around a famous person's spots to prove to you that they're real. But that's not very fair either. Often, celebrities don't ask for the media to make them look perfect. In fact, some celebrities get very cross that images of them are changed.

Get real

What's funny is those unreal versions of people in cartoons or photographs would find it really hard to live in the real world. The girls would be so tall, their bodies so thin and their heads and eyes so big, they'd find it hard to stand upright. The boys' chests would be so big, they wouldn't be able to find a shirt that fastened over their muscles.

If you *always* see boys with big muscles saving the day, never see anyone with a disability or only see one colour of skin in your favourite shows then they can make you see the world in a different way. When the world is bombarding you with perfect pictures and unreal versions of people in cartoons or photographs it helps to remember that they're not real.

Change the story

Now you understand a bit more about what's real and what's not, you have a choice: you can keep looking at the pictures served up to you each day OR you can look for your own role models. You can look at people's achievements, what they have to say and feel inspired by who people really are. Maybe they play a sport you love or are fighting for a cause you believe in. If you love a particular celebrity, look past their perfect pictures and read about who they are and how they got to where they are. You have the power to fill your mind with positive information that makes you feel good from head to toe.

Now finish this sentence.

I WILL keep it real by doing this one thing:......................................

....

....

....

....

....

it's OK to NOT FEEL OK

Helping hand

It doesn't matter who we are or what we do, at some point we're not going to feel okay. Wanting to cry or shout, stamp your feet or run away is all a normal part of being human. Some days, you're going to have a row or get scared about a test. You might find puberty tricky to deal with or get cross with your body for not doing what you want it to do. Some people experience sad or anxious feelings that can be difficult to deal with. This chapter is all about how to look after yourself when things get tough. Your mind and body are connected, and you're about to learn how to look after them both at the same time.

Get to know your feelings

If your life was a series of emojis it'd be:

A single day can contain so many different emotions. You can feel happy that you're enjoying a lovely piece of toast, annoyed that your hair won't go the right way, worried that you didn't finish a piece of homework and excited to see a friend – all before you've even left the house. Often, we feel more than one emotion at the same time. It's what makes humans amazing, but it can be exhausting when you're the one doing all of that *feeling*.

You may also find the changes that happen to your hormones in puberty bring a whole new roller coaster of emotions. Those changing feelings might seem to go into overdrive, making you furious, then sad and then really happy. You could find it difficult to know what you really feel from one minute to the next. The best way to deal with all of these feelings is to let yourself feel them. It might seem scary to feel sad or anxious and scared. But the first step to feeling happy is to make friends with all of your emotions. Listen to yourself and accept how you feel right now.

Why we have difficult feelings

Some feelings fly past quickly (like that annoyed feeling you get when someone skips a queue). But other feelings move in to our bodies for longer. These can be brought on by big events, like puberty, an exam, or a new school or by everyday stress like falling out with a friend, worrying about how we look, or experiencing a form of bullying.

Some negative feelings seem to come from nowhere. We might feel anxious but we don't know why. Some people feel very sad for a long time and they're not sure what caused it. This can be a type of illness called depression.

What is depression?

Depression is a real illness with real symptoms. These range from feelings of unhappiness and hopelessness to losing interest in the things you used to enjoy and feeling very tearful. There can be physical symptoms, too, such as feeling constantly tired, sleeping badly, having no appetite and various aches and pains.

Depression can happen to anyone – even people you might not expect it to, like your favourite celebrities. Selena Gomez, Zayn Malik, Harry Potter author J.K. Rowling and Prince Harry are all very open about their struggle with depression.

The good news is that with the right treatment and support, most people with depression can make a good recovery, and as these famous people prove, it doesn't have to hold you back.

Let it go

It's important to take the time to get to know how you're feeling and give your emotions room to breathe so they can do what they need to do.

We often think of people crying when they're sad, laughing when they're happy or shouting when they're mad. In fact, the way we react to emotions is less simple than that. Sometimes, we cry when we're really happy or laugh when we're sad.

There's no right way to behave when you're feeling emotional. The most important thing is to allow your body to do what it needs to do. Emotions are like a flood. If we try to build a dam to keep our feelings inside, we can end up making ourselves feel ill. There's nothing wrong or silly about crying. It doesn't matter if you're a toddler or a footballer, a grandma or a dad, no one should try to bottle up their feelings up.

Talk it out

When it comes to letting out your feelings, nothing beats sharing them. That's why there's a lot of advice in this book about finding someone you trust to talk to. Feelings can be overwhelming. They can stop us thinking rationally and they can make us lose sight of what's really going on. It doesn't matter if it's a parent, sibling, a favourite teacher, an aunt you've always had a special bond with or your friends – talking to someone you trust is the best way to help you work out how you feel and to get help.

If you really feel you can't talk to someone you know, there are other people who can help, too. Turn to page 158 for a list of websites and phone numbers you can call to speak to people in confidence about your worries.

But what should I say?

While talking IS the best way to help your feelings, it can also be the most difficult. Have you ever really wanted to talk to someone, but couldn't find the right words to start the conversation? It's almost like the stage fright you feel before speaking in front of your whole class, except this is with one other person. The more you think about opening your mouth, the more the words escape you. Deciding to talk to someone is a great choice, so even though it may feel tricky to get started, here are some tips to help you to get the conversation started.

Try saying....

Can I talk to you?

I need some advice.

Can you help me?

If you find it hard talking to people, you could try sending a message or writing a note. You can have the whole conversation electronically, if you like, or you could just say that you'd like to talk to the person about something. That way, the person can help you start the conversation. It's much easier for them to help you by saying, **'What's up?'** than to dive in cold.

Once you've got the conversation started, it helps to open up as much as you can.

Try saying…

> **The problem is…**

> **I feel like…**

> **You can help me by doing this…**

Don't worry if your emotions take over. It takes a lot of energy to talk about how you feel. You might feel shaky, tearful, even a little embarrassed. The person you chose to tell won't mind one bit. Let them comfort you, if you want, and take the time you need before you feel ready to start talking again.

Remember, a problem shared really is a problem halved. The people you trust to share your problem with will want to help you feel better – and it doesn't matter if it takes a few hours or even a few months, they're going to want to be there to help you every step of the way.

The professionals

Sometimes, we need a little bit more help than our family or friends are able to offer. You should try to speak to someone you know first, if you feel able to. But they (or you) might decide that a counsellor is the best person to help make you feel better.

A counsellor is a person whose job it is to guide people through tricky times. That makes sense. These are people who have spent years studying and practising how to help people to talk about their emotions. They will listen, ask questions, and they will never tell anyone what you say to them.

It's worth remembering, counsellors are people, too. We might not click with the first counsellor we see. That's okay. You can ask to see someone else if you want to.

A doctor can refer you to a counsellor for therapy. There's also a website on page 158 that will help you or your parents to find counsellors in your area.

MINDFULNESS

Try mindfulness

The trick with mindfulness is to live in the here and now. Humans are always worrying about the past or future. Babies are brilliant at living in the moment but, as we grow, we forget how. You can train yourself to stop thinking and worrying by using your senses every day. You might choose to listen and look at the things around you, to listen carefully to a piece of music or to practise yoga and to feel your body moving. The aim is to listen to your senses and to empty your mind, so your worries drift away.

Mindfulness is a skill you can use every day. Try this simple activity to find out how it works.

It's important to take the time to stop rushing around and listen to yourself. Listen to your breathing. And check in with how you feel... Do you feel still or calm? Perhaps fidgety or bored? Are you feeling happy, sad, or even a little frustrated, maybe?

Now, open a window or sit outside and listen – just listen – to all of the sounds you can hear. Birds chirping or squawking, the hum of cars, the rumble of an aeroplane, leaves rustling, distant laughter, the clatter of pans – pick out every sound, and let your mind empty of any other thoughts.

Exercise helps

If you're sad, anxious, mad or worried, exercise can help. Remember those endorphins we talked about in chapter four? Exercise literally makes us smile! Plus, it helps us keep to a routine, gives us energy, and it makes our bodies happy. As long as we don't exercise too much, moving can be a really useful way of looking after ourselves when we're going through a tough time.

Exercise can also help when we're feeling anxious. Remember those inner cavepeople we met in chapter five? They're not just hanging around in our bodies affecting the food we choose. Our ancestors have a big effect on the way we feel and, you guessed it, that's because events from their past have shaped the way our brains work today.

Imagine you're a caveperson taking a walk. Suddenly, the bushes move and you think, **'Probably a bit of wind,'** and then a sabre-toothed tiger leaps out of the bushes and eats you.

It was wise for cavepeople to assume that every time a bush moved, it was a sabre-toothed tiger. They always had to fear the worst, in order to stay alive. And the same is true of humans today. We fear the worst because our brains are hardwired to think that way.

Now, let's go back to the moment when that sabre-toothed tiger popped out of the bush. Before it gobbled us up, we got a big burst of adrenaline. We had to decide, **'Should I stay or should I go?'** Adrenaline was what helped cavepeople to survive, by giving them a big push of energy so they could run away.

Nowadays, we get the same burst of adrenaline, but the stresses we face are not the same as sabre-toothed tigers. We can't out-run an exam, or sprint faster than an argument with our best mate. We still get adrenaline, but there's nowhere for it to go. That's why exercise can be useful when we're feeling stressed or angry. We can run off some of those tickly tummy feelings that come with feeling worried. We can pound the pavement or wallop a ball to get rid of the physical effects of anger.

It's important to remember that exercise isn't a cure. It isn't helpful to use exercise as a way to escape from how you feel. You can run up a mountain, but your problem will still be waiting for you when you reach the top. But you can use exercise as a way of helping you feel better while you accept and deal with how you're feeling.

It's okay to try to be happy

The same is true of any activity that makes you feel good. Once you've accepted how you feel, let your emotions out and talked to someone you trust, it can be really helpful to just have fun. Listen to your favourite band, have a laugh with your mates, take your dog for a walk, read your favourite book or have a bubble bath. Look after yourself and, remember, you will be okay.

Now finish this sentence so you know who to turn to when life gets tough.

I can deal with anything life throws my way. The people I can talk to are:……………………

……………………………………………………
……………………………………………………
……………………………………………………
……………………………………………………
……………………………………………………
……………………………………………………

the most important thing you wear is confidence!

Celebrate yourself

You're most of the way through this brilliant body confidence journey. You and your body are the best of friends – which seems like a brilliant reason to have a party! It's time to blow up the balloons, break out the banners and order a cake with your face on it (if you like) because in this chapter we're celebrating

you!

Ready, set, glow!

Remember all the way back in chapter two when you wrote down all of the things that your brilliant body does for you? Well, hopefully, after reading this book you know yourself even better than before. Growing up can be confusing – your body is going through changes and you're trying to remember to eat your five-a-day – but now we're going to look into what makes you so amazing so you can glow up and be you!

Here are some suggestions to help get you started:

> What do you really like about the way you look? Maybe you've got a big smile, a great haircut or a particularly fantastic big toe.

> What have you achieved? Maybe you did better than you expected in a test, scored a goal, read six books this holiday or got out of bed before your mum or dad told you to.

> What kind deeds have you done? Did you give advice to a friend? Help your teacher? Maybe you managed not to tease your younger sibling all day.

When did you do the right thing even though it was difficult? Did you revise really hard to get that good test result? Maybe you 'fessed up to something and it wasn't easy to be honest. Perhaps you said NO to something you didn't want to do.

What makes you a great friend? Are you a great listener? Do you make people laugh? Maybe you come up with exciting ideas? Or maybe you always know how to make other people feel happy?

Whatever you choose to write down, remember:

YOU ARE AMAZING

Now, write some awesome facts about yourself in the shapes below and let the real you shine.

Keep this page and use it to remind yourself how completely brilliant you are, inside and out.

Beauty shines from inside

Knowing how awesome you are is a great way to feel confident. Did you know that how you feel about yourself on the inside can change the way you look on the outside? Try standing in front of a mirror and let your head and shoulders slump. That's how people tend to stand when they're not feeling very confident. Now stand up straight, throw your shoulders back, lift your head up and smile. Much better, right? Even when you don't realize it, your thoughts and feelings are changing the way you appear to other people. And more than that – moving your body differently can change the way *you* feel!

How a smile goes viral!

Try picturing something that makes you smile. A fluffy puppy tripping over his paws, a funny TV episode that made you laugh out loud or your best friend pulling a daft face, maybe! You could even put on a happy song that you love. Now, let a giant grin spread from ear to ear. Can you feel your spirits lifting? Smiles are magical. Science has shown a smile can lower stress, stop us getting ill and may even help us live longer! Plus, grinning doesn't just make us feel good – we can light up a room and make others feel happy with a simple smile. That's why smiling is a great way to make new friends.

Change the record

Sometimes, it's hard to smile and, even though you're an amazing human, it can feel like an uphill struggle to be kind to yourself. There are lots of things that can affect the way you feel. Puberty could make you feel insecure about your body changing. You might feel bombarded with pictures on your phone or in magazines that make you think you should look a certain way. Changing emotions might make you row with friends or family a lot, and you might feel like you just don't know how to get on with people anymore.

If you're feeling like this, remember these are just thoughts – and you can change them. It takes a bit of practice but, just like you can change the music you're listening to, you can change the soundtrack in your mind. Next time a negative idea comes into your head, catch it and think, **'You are just a thought.'** You can even picture yourself putting the thought in to a bubble then blowing it away, and think about something positive instead.

If you think:

> I hate maths! I'm going to fail this test! My parents will be so mad!

Crumple up that thought, kick it into the air and replace it with:

> I find maths difficult, but this test is a great opportunity to learn. If I work hard and do the best I can, my parents (and I) will be proud of me.

Maybe you keep thinking:

> I keep getting so mad with my friends. There must be something wrong with me!

Parcel up that thought, send it on its way and think positively instead:

> My emotions are all over the place at the moment. But if I explain to my friends how I'm feeling, they'll think I'm amazing for being honest with them.

Look how these positive thoughts can change your actions, too. Once you get into the habit of changing your thoughts, you can turn any situation into a positive, and if you need a bit of help, just look at all of the brilliant things you've just written about yourself. There's so much to celebrate about you!

Dream big

Imagine you've got a magic telescope that lets you see into your own future. Now turn to the next page and write down what you'd like to be doing in ten years' time.

If you're struggling, write down some ideas that make you feel excited – it helps to think of the things you love most in your life. Be honest with yourself – if you love animals and science, you might want to be a vet, but if you love animals and writing, you might want to be an author who writes about animals instead. If you love singing and being centre stage, you might want to be a pop star. If you love singing, hate the limelight but love helping people, you might decide to use your talent to be a music therapist. But if you have your heart set on a pop career, you've just got to find a way to overcome your shyness so you can step on stage.

DREAM BIG

Whether you found this easy peasy or really tricky, if you don't know what you want to be when you grow up, it doesn't matter. You'll probably change your mind lots of times before then. In fact, the job you end up doing might not even exist yet. You might invent a time machine or maybe even teleportation… Who knows what the world will be like in ten years!

Your dreams are special to you. Dreaming **BIG** means finding the things that make you feel excited and then letting nothing stand in your way.

Dreams CAN come true

It's good to have dreams and goals. They can help you to work hard and to achieve great things. You should never let anyone try to stop you dreaming – and that includes you! You can be anything you want to be. You just need to believe in yourself and work hard to make your dreams happen.

Look at what you wrote down. Maybe you said you'd like to be a famous movie star, a surgeon or a world champion chess player. Turn to the next page and write down all of the things you can do **NOW** to help make that dream happen. How can you practise (and practise) the skills you'll need? It's okay if you need to ask for help, too. Your friends, family and teachers can help you on your way to achieving your dreams.

Star power

A movie star isn't born in front of the camera. Zendaya loved acting so much she took every opportunity she could to be on stage – at school and at her local theatre group. The same goes for musicians. They have to practise and practise to avoid playing a bad note. Ed Sheeran played the guitar at home and at his local church. When he wasn't playing he was listening to and being inspired by other musicians.

Your favourite stars had to come away from every audition knowing they'd given it their best shot, even if they didn't get the part. They had to have the confidence to keep going when people said no. That's how they became the best – nothing could stand in the way of their dreams.

'I would say my best decision I ever made was to pursue my dream and give it my all.' Zendaya.

'You start off with a little spark, and it's whether or not you nurture that spark. You have to expand it and work on it.' Ed Sheeran

You've got to really want it

Your dreams have to be real and they have to be yours. There's no point trying to become a world-famous ballet dancer if you hate dancing. (Did you know, ballet dancers get black toenails from standing on tiptoe on wooden blocks? Ouch!) You've got to REALLY want to dance *Swan Lake* to suffer for your art. Doctors, on the other hand, have to study their degree for five years (with even more training after that!). Then, they work one and a half times more hours than the average person. You're never going to put in that much work if you're not excited about saving lives or helping people. (Doctors and ballet dancers are officially amazing.)

Sometimes, people will get a bit too excited about your life and try to tell you what to do with it. Parents, friends, teachers – they might think they know best. They mean well, but when it comes to your life you're in charge. Only you can feel the fire you get in your belly when you're excited about something. Only you can decide whether you're willing to lose a toenail to achieve your dream. So, listen to yourself.

Those dreams are yours.

Before you dash off to the final chapter, you know what to do. Finish this sentence.

I AM amazing because:..............

....
....
....
....
....
....

BE YOURSELF, Everyone ELSE IS TAKEN

Being you begins with you

Well done for making it to the last chapter! This book has been a journey and, like all good adventures, it's had fun bits, challenges and the odd mountain to climb. This chapter is no different – we've saved the best section until last. You're going to learn how to feel confident and be true to yourself, whatever life throws at you. It'll explain how to know your own mind and to speak it. Plus, you'll find out how to spread a little happiness around you everywhere you go. Think of your body confidence as being like magic dust that can change the lives of other people. But we're getting ahead of ourselves. Let's start with the most important person – YOU!

Meet your new best friend

There's not much point knowing you're ace but never hanging out with yourself one-on-one. We know what you're thinking. **'What are you talking about? I'm with ME all the time! I go to bed with** *me, I wake up with me, I'm in my own head EVERY SECOND OF EVERY DAY!'* Which is true. But we're talking about spending quality time with you. In the same way you and your best mate might hang out together and have really cool chats and end the day feeling like you know each other a little bit better – you can do exactly the same thing with your own mind.

It's all about understanding who you are and what you think about stuff. It's about having feelings that are unique to you, which can be different from those of your friends, family or classmates. Now, you could be the kind of person who knows exactly what they think and feel about everything. But most of us flip flop all over the place when we hear the opinions of others. We might think we really like a new album then panic when someone at school says it's the worst thing they've ever heard. We decide we hate it, delete it from our playlist and blush every time someone says the name of the band. But what does this achieve? Except that we don't get to listen to some great music we liked. The problem with listening to other people is that some of them are so loud they can make it hard for us to hear our own thoughts.

Plan some ME time
••••••••••••••••••••••••••••••••••••
Often, we say yes to stuff because other people want us to. You might want to hang out with your friends, but that doesn't mean you have to skip drama class because they want to play football,

or never get to reread your favourite book because they invited you over for the fifth night in a row. I'm not saying it isn't fun to hang out with your best mates a lot – but remember to save a little bit of time for you. Just as you can say NO to doing anything that doesn't make you feel comfortable, you can also say no to create more time for you.

Go solo!

Sometimes people, even grown-ups, feel like being on their own is the worst thing in the world. They think there's no way they could go to the cinema by themselves, or that they'd rather eat worms than go out for lunch without a friend. But being on your own is brilliant! You can spend time doing anything you want to. Listen to your favourite band, paint, write a poem, hang out with your cat – just do something that makes YOU happy.

Write down one thing you love doing and one thing you'd love to try but haven't done yet:

....

....

Maybe you said football – how can you spend more time on this hobby? Can you join a local team, start your own football club with a group of friends who love football, or simply spend half an hour after school each day practising new tricks?

And now for the thing you'd love to try – how can you make it happen? Can you speak to a friend or family member? If it's expensive, could you save up your pocket money? Write down the date you'd like to achieve this by and make it happen!

Know your mind

Spending time with ourselves is an important part of getting to know what we really think and feel. If you like an album, you can listen to it over and over again, and while you're doing that, you can decide why you like it. Then, if someone says they don't, you can respect their opinion but it won't affect how you feel. Remember, every body (and every mind) is different, so we won't all like the same things.

Write something you love in the heart opposite and then write all the reasons why you love it around the heart. It might be a song, a book, a film, playing tennis or crafting. Think about how it makes you feel and why – this will help you figure out why you love it so much!

I LOVE
....
....
....

Speak your mind

Now you know your own mind, you're going to be unstoppable. When you understand your feelings and opinions, it's a lot easier to say what you think. But it can still be hard to put it into words – or to give your opinion without drowning out other people.

If you find it hard to say what you think, you might choose not to or you'll say it so quietly that no one listens. This is called being passive. Some people are very good at giving their opinion – maybe a little too good! They can come across as aggressive, which can make other people feel small. In fact, if you're aggressive, people might decide not to listen to your opinion at all.

The art of speaking your mind is like the story of Goldilocks and the three bears. Being passive is too sweet, being aggressive is too salty – you need to get it 'just right'. That means being confident and giving your opinion in a way that doesn't leave a bad taste in anyone's mouth. The trick is to listen to what other people have to say and then to give your view without saying they're wrong. It's important to know that respecting someone's opinion is different to agreeing. You can have different views and still get along.

When you're being assertive you will:

- ask questions and listen to other people's opinions
- **speak clearly**
- feel relaxed giving your point of view
- know what you think and feel so you don't trip over your words
- smile at people
- sit up straight
- seem interested in what everyone has to say

As with all new things, it can take a bit of practice. You can try speaking your mind into a mirror or even video yourself on your phone. Just like riding a bike the more you do it the easier it will become and, when you know how, you'll never forget.

The power of words

It's not just opinions that can affect how we think and feel. Even comments that seem harmless can make you feel like other people expect something from you. Imagine lots of people call you strong. You might start to feel that being strong is important, otherwise why would people say it? You might wonder what strong means exactly and change your behaviour. You might try not to cry in public or insist you're okay when you're not. Likewise, if someone calls you pretty all the time, you might think that being pretty is more important than having an opinion. Maybe you start to worry more if you're having a bad hair day or if you wake up with a spot on the end of your nose. Of course, it's lovely to get a compliment. If you know yourself, you can feel good without letting other people's words shape who you are.

Who are you anyway?

People are unique and they are changeable, too. Throughout the day your mood will vary from raring to go to super sleepy or really cheery to sudden gloom. This is why it's so useful to know the real you.

Circle all of the words that describe you:

kind

clever

energetic

arty

sporty

creative

a problem solver

strong

successful

hard-working

thoughtful

funny

talkative

calm

organized

excitable

a thinker

messy

a doer

a daydreamer

Now keep this page and come back to it whenever you need reminding of who you are! You can even come back and add more words when you discover something new about yourself.

Spread a little happiness

You're about to close this book and go out into the world feeling confident from head to toe. Wouldn't it be amazing if you could make your happiness rub off on other people? Well, guess what? You can! Remember your superpower that we talked about way back in chapter three? That's right – **KINDNESS**! Try these five acts of kindness with your friends and loved ones and you'll leave a trail of happy people who feel more confident – because of you!

I love your style! You're so funny! You're a great friend!

Pay a simple, honest compliment to make someone feel great. Tell your best friends why they're special and why they mean a lot to you. Remind them these special qualities are unique to them – because everybody is different.

Thanks for listening, for helping me, for making me feel loved.

People do brilliant stuff for you all the time. Thank a friend for listening, a teacher for helping or a parent for caring and make them feel amazing. Remember, when people feel loved they feel more confident.

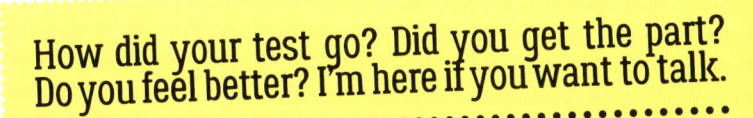

How did your test go? Did you get the part? Do you feel better? I'm here if you want to talk.

It's easy to get caught up in the drama of our own lives but if we remember the big stuff that other people have going on, and ask them about it, it shows we care. If a friend or family member seems down, let them know you're there for them.

Let's walk to class, get lunch, hang out after school.

School can be tough when you're on your own. You could try talking to someone at school who looks like they might be lonely. You'll raise their self-esteem and you might make a new friend.

Do you want to go for walk? Play tennis? Try yoga in the park?

Encourage a friend to try an activity with you that will boost their energy and make their body feel brilliant. Finish off the session with refreshing watermelon or sweet nectarine to make you both feel great inside and out.

Congratulations!

You've completed your body confidence journey. Let's recap on the amazing things you've achieved:

☐ You and your body are best friends.

☐ You've thanked your body for helping you do the things that make you happy every day.

☐ You've met your inner caveperson (cool!) and given your body the exercise and food it needs to be brilliant.

☐ You respect yourself and others and don't let other people put you down.

☐ You know kindness is a superpower and you use it to make you – and others – feel confident.

☐ You know where to turn to when you need help and you're there for your friends and family.

- [ ] You're web wise, social media smart and know how to keep it real.
- [ ] You know yourself inside out and are true to yourself whatever life throws at you.

Be you!

Remember, YOU are the star of your life and you are AMAZING! That doesn't mean you won't have ups and downs. No one is perfect and, like all of us, you will make mistakes. But you'll love and laugh and live in YOUR unique body. You have the power to do anything and be anything you want to be. So get out there and be

you!

Before you go and grab your dreams, finish these sentences.

I have confidence because:
....
....

I am strong because:
....
....

I am wise because:
....
....

I am powerful because:
....
....

Ready, set, GLOW!

Glossary

balanced diet: eating lots of different types of foods that give the body a variety of health benefits.

body confidence: accepting and feeling happy with how you look and what your body can do.

bully: a person who deliberately hurts someone else to make themselves feel more powerful than them. Bullying can be physical or emotional. (See cyberbullying, below.)

compliment: a kind comment that tells someone something positive about how they look, what they do or who they are.

counsellor: a professional who is trained to give people advice and to help them deal with difficult emotions. This could be because of relationship difficulties, grief or to help them deal with everyday life.

cyberbullying: bullying that takes place via electronic communication, such as social media or text messages. (See bullying, above.)

depression: a serious medical condition that makes people feel sad, hopeless or lose interest in things they used to enjoy. The symptoms may persist for weeks or months and are bad enough to interfere with everyday life.

diversity: understanding every person is unique and has value regardless of race, ethnicity, sex, gender, age, mental and physical abilities and religious beliefs.

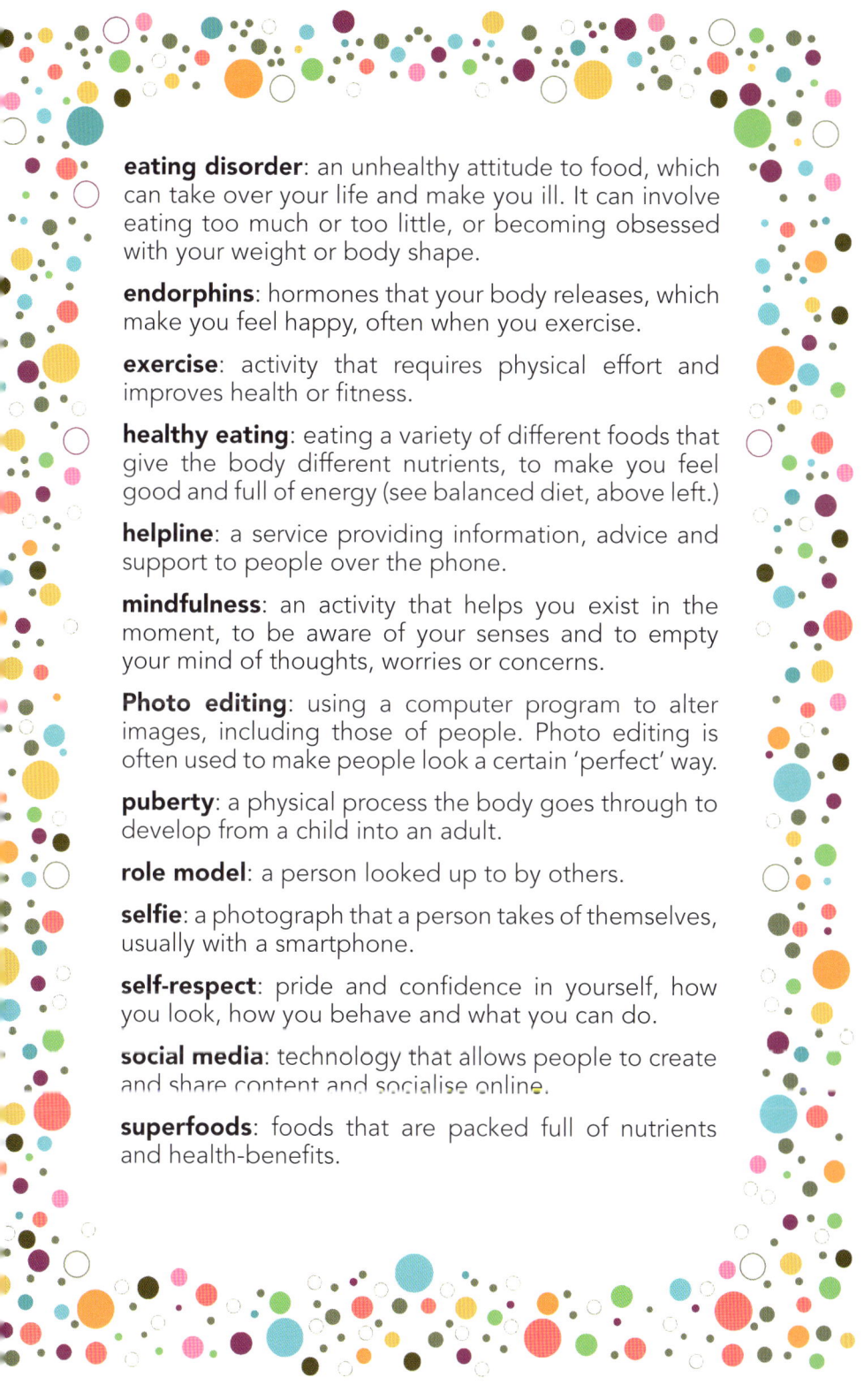

eating disorder: an unhealthy attitude to food, which can take over your life and make you ill. It can involve eating too much or too little, or becoming obsessed with your weight or body shape.

endorphins: hormones that your body releases, which make you feel happy, often when you exercise.

exercise: activity that requires physical effort and improves health or fitness.

healthy eating: eating a variety of different foods that give the body different nutrients, to make you feel good and full of energy (see balanced diet, above left.)

helpline: a service providing information, advice and support to people over the phone.

mindfulness: an activity that helps you exist in the moment, to be aware of your senses and to empty your mind of thoughts, worries or concerns.

Photo editing: using a computer program to alter images, including those of people. Photo editing is often used to make people look a certain 'perfect' way.

puberty: a physical process the body goes through to develop from a child into an adult.

role model: a person looked up to by others.

selfie: a photograph that a person takes of themselves, usually with a smartphone.

self-respect: pride and confidence in yourself, how you look, how you behave and what you can do.

social media: technology that allows people to create and share content and socialise online.

superfoods: foods that are packed full of nutrients and health-benefits.

Index

being
    amazing 10, 11, 13, 19, 24, 63, 64, 81, 97, 110, 124, 129, 130, 137, 150, 151
    kind 12, 23, 27, 28, 31–49, 51, 64, 93, 124, 129, 147
    normal 20, 22, 98, 104, 109
    true to yourself 12, 81–95, 139, 151
    unique 8, 16, 18, 42, 58, 77, 140, 146
    you 139–52

body, your 10, 15–29, 63, 123, 124, 128, 129, 139, 150, 154, 160
    adrenaline 119–20
    confidence 11, 123, 139, 150, 154
    endorphins 51–2, 119, 155
    puberty 20–3, 32, 33, 91, 109, 111, 129, 155,
    respecting your 27–8, 31, 47, 155

bullying 12, 36–42, 111, 154, 160
    cyberbullying 46, 154, 160
    myths 40–1
    standing up to 33, 38–9

cavepeople 71–2, 73, 119
celebs 20, 32, 97, 104–5, 112

emotions 70, 109–21, 129, 130, 154
    anger 120
    confidence 11, 12, 27, 48, 54, 128, 139, 144, 148, 150, 152, 155
    difficult 27, 109, 111, 154
    depression 111, 112, 154
    frustration 118
    happiness 26, 31, 54, 66, 74, 85, 110, 111, 112, 113, 118, 119, 121, 125, 128, 129, 141, 148, 150, 155
    insecurity 32, 88, 129
    positivity 57, 107, 129, 131
    sadness 22, 35, 37, 42, 93, 109, 111, 112, 113, 118, 119,

exercise 51–60, 81, 119, 120, 150, 155
    athletes, amazing 58–60
    moving 15, 23, 28, 51, 54–6, 57, 66, 117, 119, 128
    sports 8, 26, 53, 54, 55, 56, 60, 107, 147

food and healthy eating
14, 63–79, 81, 119, 150, 154, 155, 160
alternative diets 68
comfort food 70
eating disorders 78, 154, 160
fats 63, 66, 71, 73
fruit and vegetables 66, 67, 68, 69, 77
protein 64, 65, 66, 67
salt 71, 73, 74
sugar 69, 71, 73
super foods 64–5, 66
water 67, 68–9

friendships 18, 40, 42, 81–95
ending 91–3
falling out 87–90
fixing 89–90
new 94
respect 48, 51, 81, 90, 93, 142
self-respect 48, 150, 155
staying true to yourself 81
your squad 81–2, 85, 86

hobbies 15, 18, 26, 94, 142

mind 15, 26, 63, 64, 74 5, 76, 87, 102, 107, 109, 117–8, 129, 139–152, 155
dreams 12, 131–4, 136, 152
know your 87, 139
mindfulness 117–8, 155
memory 25–6

positive thinking 57, 107, 129, 131
speak your 144–6

online life
image, protect your 98–9
Internet 436
photos, edited 102, 104–5, 106, 155
real, keep it 11, 97–107, 107, 151
safe surfing 44–5
social media 11, 46, 98–103, 151, 154, 155, 160
selfies 155

role models 107, 155

skills 18, 26, 58, 133
solo, going 141
star power 135–6

talking 12, 13, 23, 32–3, 39, 70, 78, 89, 90, 93, 94, 113–6, 121, 149, 160
about problems 23, 121, 113–6
asking for help 12, 39, 78, 89, 114–5
compliments 13, 146, 148 9, 154
no, how to say 86–7, 141
professional, talk to 116, 154, 160
words, power of 146

157

Where to find help

BBC Advice: BBC Advice presented by Radio 1, 1Xtra and BBC Switch gives you the straight facts on teen issues from bullying to sexual health.

www.bbc.co.uk/radio1/advice/your_body/boys_bodies

www.bbc.co.uk/radio1/advice/your_body/girls_bodies

Beat: if you or anyone you know needs help with an eating disorder or any other difficulties with food, weight or shape, this charity has lots of advice and support – including a helpline.

www.beateatingdisorders.org.uk

Childline: Childline is there for you if you need to talk or any support.

www.childline.org.uk

Ditch the Label: check out Ditch the Label for help and advice on bullying and cyberbullying

www.ditchthelabel.org

Mind: a mental health charity, with tons of useful information online.

www.mind.org.uk

National Society for the Prevention of Cruelty to Children (NSPCC): a charity fighting to end child abuse, it has lots of information on its website.

www.nspcc.org.uk

Net Aware: this NSPCC website has information about social media sites, including how suitable they are for young people, and contact details that can be used to stop cyberbullying.

www.net-aware.org.uk

Samaritans: the Samaritans offer a safe place for you to talk any time you like, about anything at all.

www.samaritans.org

YoungMinds: a charity helping young people to improve their mental health. It has a confidential helpline for parents who might be worried about a child or young person.

youngminds.org.uk